ABOUT THIS STUDY:

Now, more than ever, people are feeling a gaping hole where authentic relationships should be. It's not that we don't know lots of people. In fact, with school, church, cell phones, and social networking we've got more access to each other than any generation has ever had in the history of the world. How many "friends" do you have?

But in the middle of all of this "connection" everybody seems to be deeply lonely. At the heart level, everybody seems to think they are on their own. As much as we really want authentic relationships, we're not willing to do what it takes to have them... to own up to our personal issues that stand in the way of healthy relationships. We're too proud, scared and selfish to admit that we need help from God and people. We settle for fake relationships because it's easier.

Psalm 32 goes there. To have authentic relationships we need to be authentic with God and with each other. This study will challenge you to deal with that simple fact. Take an intentional step toward a life full of authentic relationships.

AUTHENTIC

PSALM 32

ontrack devotions
EXPEDITION

www.OnTrackDevotions.com

OnTrack Expedition: Authentic: Psalm 32

Printed in the United States of America

Author: Joshua D. Wilhite
Executive Developer: Benjamin J. Wilhite
Graphic design by Lance Young (higherrockcreative.com)

ISBN-13 978-0692478639
ISBN 0692478639

10 9 8 7 6 5 4 3 2 1

PSALM 32 (ESV)

Of David. A Maskill.

1 **Blessed is the one**
    whose transgression is forgiven,
    whose sin is covered.
2 **Blessed is the man**
    against whom the LORD counts no iniquity,
    and in whose spirit there is no deceit.

3 **For when I kept silent,**
    my bones wasted away through my groaning all day long.
4   For day and night your hand was heavy upon me;
        my strength was dried up as by the heat of summer.
        Selah
5 **I acknowledged my sin to you,**
    and I did not cover my iniquity.
        I said, "I will confess my transgressions to the LORD,"
        and you forgave the iniquity of my sin.
        Selah

6 **Therefore let everyone who is godly offer prayer to you at a time when you may be found;**
    surely in the rush of great waters, they shall not reach him.
7   You are a hiding place for me;
    you preserve me from trouble;
    you surround me with shouts of deliverance.
    Selah

8 I will **instruct** you
    and **teach** you in the way you should go;
  I will **counsel** you
    with my eye upon you.

9 **Be not like a horse or a mule,**
    without understanding
    which must be curbed with bit and bridle,
    or it will not stay near you.
10 **Many are the sorrows of the wicked,**
    but steadfast love surrounds the one who trusts in the LORD.
11 Be glad in the LORD, and rejoice, O righteous,
    and shout for joy, all you upright in heart!

PASSAGE
INTRO NOTES

Record key ideas from the passage introduction or from your first read through the entire passage. Write down any "big questions" on the tag below so you can revisit them during the week.

ocd
EXPEDITION

BIG questions this week...

1: SET GOALS

This exercise is designed to help prepare your heart and mind for the week of your upcoming event. Take some time to get alone and answer them. Good goals should be specific and measurable.

(1) Complete the following sentences to help you formulate some goals for the week:

This week, I hope I...

This week, I hope we as a group...

(2) Complete the following sentences to help you begin to formulate a strategy for seeing the above goals fulfilled:

In light of my answers above, I must...

In light of my answers above, we must...

(3) Complete the following sentences to help you formulate a plan to avoid what will derail your goals:

In light of my answers, I must not...

In light of my answers, we must not...

2: PLAN & COMMIT

Take your responses from the previous questions and write out a "personal commitment" for the week. That is, what are you going to personally commit to be doing this week and commit to not be doing. You will sign it and seek out at least one other person on the trip who will read it, pray for its fulfillment, and keep you accountable to it. If possible, seek out a second witness that will not be part of the event group that will pray for you during the event and will check in with you afterward to see how it went.

I, _____, personally commit to

I further commit to not

Name: _____

Signature: _____

Witness#1: _____

Witness#2: _____

Date: ___/___/___

1: JOURNAL

Experiences
What experiences have you faced in the last 24 hours?

Questions
What questions do you find yourself asking?

Conclusions
What kind of conclusions are you coming to about yourself and others?

 otd
EXPEDITION

2: READ PSALM 32
Read the entire Psalm with a specific focus on verses 1 and 2.

3: EVALUATE
Answer the questions below based on today's reading focus.

Verses 1 and 2 both start with the word, "blessed." Why is it such a blessing to have your sins forgiven?

How certain are you that your sins are forgiven?

Circle One: Forgiven for sure 1 2 3 4 5 6 7 8 9 10 Not sure at all

What do you think it means in verse 2 to have no deceit in your spirit?

How honest are you about your sin? Do you ever think about how your actions affect other people and God?

Verse 1 is almost exactly the same as verse 2 except for the very last line. What's the connection between having a spirit with no deceit and having your sins forgiven?

4: INTEGRATE
Spend some time on each of the following activities to get the most out of today's study.

Memorize Psalm 32:1-2

Pray
Spend some time praying for yourself and for others in your group.

Commit
In light of what you see in yourself so far, what personal commitment will you make for today? Write it down...

Today, I'm praying for...

I commit to...

2ND DAY
COVER-UP

1: JOURNAL

Experiences
What experiences have you faced in the last 24 hours?

Questions
What questions do you find yourself asking?

Conclusions
What kind of conclusions are you coming to about yourself and others?

2: READ PSALM 32
Read the entire Psalm with a specific focus on verses 1 and 2.

OtD
EXPEDITION

3: EVALUATE
Answer the questions below based on today's reading focus.

Verses 1 and 2 both start with the word, "blessed." Why is it such a blessing to have your sins forgiven?

How certain are you that your sins are forgiven?

Circle One: Forgiven for sure 1 2 3 4 5 6 7 8 9 10 Not sure at all

What do you think it means in verse 2 to have no deceit in your spirit?

How honest are you about your sin? Do you ever think about how your actions affect other people and God?

Verse 1 is almost exactly the same as verse 2 except for the very last line. What's the connection between having a spirit with no deceit and having your sins forgiven?

4: INTEGRATE
Spend some time on each of the following activities to get the most out of today's study.

Memorize Psalm 32:1-2
Pray
Spend some time praying for yourself and for others in your group.

Commit
In light of what you see in yourself so far, what personal commitment will you make for today? Write it down...

Today, I'm praying for...

I commit to...

1: JOURNAL

Experiences
What experiences have you faced in the last 24 hours?

Questions
What questions do you find yourself asking?

Conclusions
What kind of conclusions are you coming to about yourself and others?

2: READ PSALM 32
Read the entire Psalm with a specific focus on verses 1 and 2.

O+d
EXPEDITION

3: EVALUATE
Answer the questions below based on today's reading focus.

What do verses 6 and 7 tell us about God's attitude toward the people He's forgiven?

What does it mean for God to be your "hiding place?"

What are some of the difficult things in your life that you sometimes want to hide from?

David went through lots of tough times while he followed God. God didn't make his troubles go away all the time. What do you think David meant in verse 7 when he wrote that God would protect him from trouble?

How can praying to God help with life's troubles?

4: INTEGRATE
Spend some time on each of the following activities to get the most out of today's study.

Memorize Psalm 32:1-2

Pray
Spend some time praying for yourself and for others in your group.

Commit
In light of what you see in yourself so far, what personal commitment will you make for today? Write it down...

Today, I'm praying for...

I commit to...

![4TH DAY LISTEN]

1: JOURNAL

Experiences
What experiences have you faced in the last 24 hours?

Questions
What questions do you find yourself asking?

Conclusions
What kind of conclusions are you coming to about yourself and others?

2: READ PSALM 32
Read the entire Psalm with a specific focus on verses 1 and 2.

3: EVALUATE
Answer the questions below based on today's reading focus.

Verse 8 uses four different action words (verbs) that all mean pretty much the same thing. Can you list them?

What has your attitude been toward the people God has put in your life to teach you important lessons?

David was a king in Israel who had been through a lot of crazy experiences. Can you list any you might have heard about?

How credible do you think David is to teach you important lessons about God?

Circle One: Not at all 1 2 3 4 5 6 7 8 9 10 The best

What can you do to become somebody who is willing to listen to the people God has put in your life to teach you important lessons?

4: INTEGRATE
Spend some time on each of the following activities to get the most out of today's study.

Memorize Psalm 32:1-2

Pray
Spend some time praying for yourself and for others in your group.

Commit
In light of what you see in yourself so far, what personal commitment will you make for today? Write it down...

Today, I'm praying for...

I commit to...

5TH DAY
STUBBORN

1: JOURNAL

Experiences
What experiences have you faced in the last 24 hours?

Questions
What questions do you find yourself asking?

Conclusions
What kind of conclusions are you coming to about yourself and others?

2: READ PSALM 32
Read the entire Psalm with a specific focus on verses 1 and 2.

OⲦd
EXPEDITION

3: EVALUATE

Answer the questions below based on today's reading focus.

Why don't horses or mules come to their masters unless they are forced to?

Read verses 3-4 again in light of the mule in verse 9. How was David like the mule and God like the mule's owner?

Read verses 5-7 again in light of the "man who trusts" in verse 10. What did David do to stop being a "mule" and start experiencing God's love?

Based on your actions, are you more like the mule (in verse 9) or are you more like the one who trusts God (in verse 10)?

What are some things you can do to follow God instead of resisting Him like a mule?

4: INTEGRATE

Spend some time on each of the following activities to get the most out of today's study.

Memorize Psalm 32:1-2

Pray
Spend some time praying for yourself and for others in your group.

Commit
In light of what you see in yourself so far, what personal commitment will you make for today? Write it down...

Today, I'm praying for...

I commit to...

1: EVALUATE

This exercise is designed to help discover and record the key takeaways from the week. Take some time to work through the process so you will get the most out of it.

(1) Take some time to read back through the pre trip contract you signed at the beginning of the week.

Write down some of the occasions where you fulfilled your commitment this week.

Write down some of the occasions where you struggled with your commitment this week.

List some of the experiences God used this week to challenge you in light of your commitment.

(2) Read back through your daily journal entries and Bible study notes and answer the questions below.

What's the biggest thing you learned about being authentic this week?

How authentic were you with God when you came into this trip?

Circle one: Not at all 1 2 3 4 5 6 7 8 9 10 Totally

How authentic are you with God now?

Circle one: Not at all 1 2 3 4 5 6 7 8 9 10 Totally

What's keeping you from taking another step toward a deeper relationship with God?

How authentic were you with people when you came into this trip?

Circle one: Not at all 1 2 3 4 5 6 7 8 9 10 Totally

How authentic are you with people now?

Circle one: Not at all 1 2 3 4 5 6 7 8 9 10 Totally

What's keeping you from taking another step toward deeper relationships with people?

2: APPLY

This exercise is designed to help connect your key takeaways to "real life" at home.
Take some time to work through each of the steps below.

(1) Take a minute and think about what things will be like when you get home. Write down your thoughts.

What are you most looking forward to?

What are you least looking forward to?

(2) Where do you think it'll be most difficult to live out what you've learned?

(3) Where do you think it will be easiest to live out what you've learned?

OCD
EXPEDITION

3: COMMIT

Take your responses from the previous questions and write out a "personal commitment" for your transition to "real life." That is, what are you going to personally commit to be doing and commit to not be doing at home. You will sign it and seek out at least one other person from the trip who will read it, pray for its fulfillment, and keep you accountable to it. Also seek out a key person at home to share your commitment(s) with that will encourage you, pray for you and hold you accountable.

I, _____, personally commit to

I further commit to not

Name: _____

Signature: _____

Witness#1: _____

Witness#2: _____

Date: ____/____/____

MEET THE AUTHOR

Joshua Wilhite grew up in a wilderness ministry environment. He spent 10 summers working with Pilgrimage in a variety of roles and loving every minute of it. After graduating from Baptist Bible College he spent two years working as the Therapeutic Activities Coordinator at a school for troubled youth. He then spent two years working as the outfitting director for Pilgrimage. From there he transitioned to a role as a representative for Baptist Bible College visiting and speaking at over 200 churches and schools. While travelling he earned an MA in Organizational Leadership from Baptist Bible Seminary.

Since 2006 he has been serving as the Pastor of Student Ministries at Solid Rock Bible Church in Plymouth, Michigan. He oversees children's ministry, middle school, high school, and college. Josh is married with three daughters and a little white dog named Brutus (for the girls of course).

Josh has a real passion for authentic growth through discipleship and teaching. He believes that there's nothing more powerful for the teaching of God's word than real life, long-term relationships in a local church. To that end, you'll find him doing his best to help people interact with the Living God one conversation at a time.

Joshua Wilhite

Role: Pastor of Student Ministries

Where: Solid Rock Bible Church (Plymouth, MI)

Family: Married w/3 daughters

Online:
www.SolidRockPlymouth.org

OGD
EDITION

"One of the most effective tools for changing lives I have ever seen... the perfect environment for God to work resulting in permanent life change."

WILDERNESS INSTITUTE FOR LEADERSHIP DEVELOPMENT

W.I.L.D.

SIMPLYPILGRIM.COM

THE ONTRACK DEVOTIONS MILITARY EDITION IS A 12-MONTH STUDY THROUGH THE NEW TESTAMENT AND PROVERBS WRITTEN FOR TODAY'S MILITARY PERSONNEL. THE INCLUDED USER GUIDE WALKS THE READER THROUGH THE BASIC STEPS OF INDUCTIVE BIBLE STUDY (OBSERVATION, INTERPRETATION, APPLICATION, IMPLEMENTATION), ALLOWING THEM TO START AT THEIR CURRENT SKILL LEVEL AND DIVE INTO THE MEAT OF THE WORD OF GOD.

WHETHER YOU ARE A CHAPLAIN LOOKING FOR RESOURCES FOR YOUR UNIT, A CHURCH WITH ACTIVE DUTY MEMBERS OR A SOLDIER, SAILOR, AIRMAN OR MARINE THAT NEEDS A FIELD-READY DEVOTIONAL GUIDE, MOTD FITS THE BILL. THE YEAR IS BROKEN DOWN INTO 12 ONE-MONTH SECTIONS WITH A USER GUIDE THAT INTRODUCES THE "WHY" AND "HOW" OF INDUCTIVE BIBLE STUDY.

FOLLOW AND LIKE MILITARY DEVOS FOR DAILY DEVO THOUGHTS:

@MILITARYDEVOS

FACEBOOK.COM/MILITARYDEVOS

MILITARYDEVOTIONAL.COM

PILGRIMAGE EDUCATIONAL RESOURCES
1362 FORDS POND RD
CLARKS SUMMIT, PA 18411

www.ingramcontent.com/pod-product-compliance
Lightning Source LLC
Chambersburg PA
CBHW060550030426
42337CB00021B/4525